FIELD NOTES

1-8

a continuing poem

The Collected Poetry of

ROBERT KROETSCH

Beaufort Books, Inc.

New York   Toronto

FIRST PUBLISHED IN 1981 BY
Beaufort Books, Inc.

LIBRARY OF CONGRESS CATALOGUING IN PUBLICATION DA

Kroetsch, Robert, 1927-
  Field Notes

  I. Title.
PR9199.3.K7A17 1981   811'.54   81-2635
ISBN 0-8253-0074-6   AACR2

COVER ILLUSTRATION BY   ISBN 0-8253-0074-6
MAUREEN HEEL-HENDERSON   FIRST PRINTING
DESIGN BY E.J. CARSON   PRINTED AND BOUND IN CANA

Contents

Acknowledgements

'Stone Hammer Poem' appeared in *The Stone Hammer Poems*, Oolichan Books, Lantzville, B.C., 1975; second edition, 1976.

'The Ledger' was first published in book form by Applegarth Follies, London, Ont, 1975; second edition, Brick/Nairn, Ilderton, Ont, 1979.

'Seed Catalogue' and 'How I Joined the Seal Herd' appeared in *Seed Catalogue*, Turnstone Press, Winnipeg, 1977; second edition, 1979.

'The Sad Phoenician' and 'The Silent Poet Sequence' appeared in *The Sad Phoenician*, Coach House Press, Toronto, 1979.

'Sketches of a Lemon' appeared in *The Malahat Review*, Number 54, April 1980.

Preface

Traditionally, the naming of a poet — his introduction — presents a primal moment of instruction. It re-affirms all the major humanistic priorities: time, language, being, origins. The poetic character incarnated, introduced, enacted or re-enacted becomes splendour, solemnity, cunning. But to invoke the name in this manner makes very large claims: that we are written or even re-written or even, such is the dialectic of modern writing, unwritten. What some call 'the *aphrodades*,' that time 'dismal and unlucky... upon which the dead return to inhabit their former houses,' comes upon us, when we seek to turn away so we become invisible, imitated by our predecessors. In the language of criticism or *reading*, something sinister as well as splendid exists in the tradition of literature, poetry, the poetic existence.

To introduce a poet: Mr. Kroetsch, your reader, Reader, Mr. Kroetsch. 'But I thought,' remarks the reader, 'that all poets were mythical beings.' 'If you'll believe in me, I'll believe in you,' replies the poet. Of course, the point is that Robert Kroetsch is a mythical being, a self-created, quite wonderful self-made myth of a man constantly disappearing into his own laughter as his self-made world (yours to) destructs repeatedly. His writing offers a startling series of affirmations by denial, denial by affirmation, his career a series of paradoxes. Despite his under-cutting of the claims of traditional literate creativity, he has become a creative force of stunning power in a regional centre. His powerful poetics of western Canadian writing derives from eastern and American sources: Al Purdy, William Carlos Williams, Wallace Stevens. An articulate theorist of silence, he is a compulsive talker and teller of tales, an editor of a post-modern journal of poetics espousing theories of destructive poetics. His achievements, considerable as they are, have been only partially understood for the simple reason that his aim is evidently to prevent the realization that would complete his project: to keep on talking, writing the poem.

Not surprisingly, his career presents an inversion. Canadian poets tend to turn into novelists (Ondaatje, Atwood, Bowering). Novelists rarely reveal themselves as poets. But this is what Kroetsch has done in mid career. Beginning and continuing with novels, each increasingly dazzling in performance, along the way he began to publish poems and to unite them, paradoxically, by unlinking them through contrast and juxtaposition. Discontinuity as continuity. The title poem of *The Stone Hammer Poems* serves as the prologue to the present volume. He followed this first book with *The Ledger*, the *Seed Catalogue* and as part of that book 'Why I Joined the Seal Herd.' At this point, it seems, he conceived the notion that his poetry was forming itself into what he has since called his 'vasty project,' a continuing poem of which the first eight parts form the present *Field Notes*, all that he includes to date of the yet incomplete work, now comprising, in addition to the prologue, the two long works, and 'The Seal Herd,' a third long poem, *The Sad Phoenician* and four sequences or longish poems, 'The Silent Poet Sequence,' 'The Winnipeg Zoo,' 'Sketches of a Lemon,' and 'The Criminal Intensities of Love as Paradise.'

We have not had such an endeavour before, at least not in this country, though it is true that the long poem forms part of our Canadian tradition, as Michael Ondaatje reminds us in his *The Long Poem Anthology*. The *long* poem, not just the narrative, of which Northrop Frye has written, not the documentary, of which Dorothy Livesay has much to say, but something big enough to hold the world and time, a space for the vast geography, a time for the hidden history of Canada. And pushed along by what? What keeps it going? Not vasty time or history. It is those from which Kroetsch wishes to escape. Not space, though it spins out tales. Not even self, that binding-bound being. Why, then, it can only be *nothing* or rather *words* that propel it. The mystification to be disclosed, discovered, uncovered, unhidden. His coy mistress, his muse: 'though we cannot make our sun / Stand still, yet we will make him run.'

Out of an infinite number of poetic possibilities, the reader of *Field Notes* will probably notice three in particular: 1) structure; 2) voice; 3) parody. The kind of poet at work here is a poet who puts things in order, in order to create disorder: 'just one more

truth, one more / Element in the immense disorder of truths,' as
Wallace Stevens says. The order of Kroetsch's poetry is what we
now call structural: binary systems, two lines in opposition
resolved by a third; or two columns: debit/ credit. Balanced? As
in *The Ledger*. But this orderly poet is wildly disorderly. 'To hell
with the left hand margin,' he says. Part of his concern is then to
discern structures (tradition, for example), part to destroy them,
so that we may see what is *really* there. Nothing at all? What we
made up? He may very well be the one Canadian writer who
created a literary tradition by destroying it.

And voice. You hear Bob Kroetsch telling stories, not writing
poems. The field is where (how) it grows, where it dies, where it
takes place: ground, open field, field force, field games, the place
defined in its telling. The double place of self and other, body and
spirit, man and woman. And talking of that: then there was the
woman from. The double voice of that comic spiller of tales or
speller of kells or teller of spills. The antiphonal endless story of
love and death, truth and lies. Each story, in other words (and
there are always other words), tells another story. The poem is
continuing because it cannot end. There is a stone that is a colour
that is a stone:

> I have to/ I want
> to know (not know)
> ? WHAT HAPPENED

What happens is: 'You must see/ the confusion again.' There is a
book: a life, a lie. There is a lie, a tale, a sale, a sailor. How do you
grow a poet? The tales spin out, spill out, spelled out.

And parody: Ann Mandel speaks of Kroetsch's fiction where
'Characters exist within each other's fictions in classic Borgesian
confusion about who is writing and who is being written. The
role of the author as creator and recorder of human knowledge is
mocked ...' Parody: recursiveness – the story told again as its
own double where up is down, beginning is ending, everywhere
is nowhere.

The naming of the poet is sacred, exalted. Reader, meet Mr.
Kroetsch. But everything high is low, everything spiritual gross.
Mr. Kroetsch meet the reader. We have been introduced. We

know one another. Our world, the west, this country, our lives; they have their being. It didn't come to very much, after all. Or did it?

The naming of the poet. Out of nothing: something. The poem. *Continuing.*

Eli Mandel
1981

especially
for my sister,
Sheila

'Before meeting you I was vainly trying to finish a long poem.'
— HUBERT AQUIN, *Prochain Episode*

Stone

Hammer

Poem

Stone Hammer Poem

1.

This stone
become a hammer
of stone, this maul

is the colour
of bone (no,
bone is the colour
of this stone maul).

The rawhide loops
are gone, the
hand is gone, the
buffalo's skull
is gone;

the stone is
shaped like the skull
of a child.

2.

This paperweight on my desk

where I begin
this poem   was

found in a wheatfield
lost (this hammer,
this poem).

Cut to a function,
this stone was
(the hand is   gone —

3.

Grey, two-headed,
the pemmican maul

fell from the travois or
a boy playing   lost it in
the prairie wool or
a squaw   left it in
the brain of a buffalo or

It is a million
years older than
the hand that
chipped stone or
raised slough
water (or blood) or

4.

This stone maul
was found.

In the field
my grandfather
thought
was his

my father
thought was his

5.

It is a stone
old as the last
Ice Age, the
retreating/ the
recreating ice,
the retreating
buffalo, the
retreating Indians

(the saskatoons bloom
white (infrequently
the chokecherries the
highbush cranberries the
pincherries bloom
white along the barbed
wire fence (the
pemmican   winter

6.

This stone maul
stopped a plow
long enough for one
Gott im Himmel.

The Blackfoot (the
Cree?) not

finding the maul
cursed.

?did he curse
?did he try to
go back
?what happened
I have to/ I want
to know (not know)
?WHAT HAPPENED

7.

The poem
is the stone
chipped and hammered
until it is shaped
like the stone
hammer, the maul.

8.

Now the field is
mine because
I gave it
(for a price)

to a young man
(with a growing son)
who did not

notice that the land
did not belong

to the Indian who
gave it to the Queen
(for a price) who
gave it to the CPR
(for a price) which
gave it to my grandfather
(for a price) who
gave it to my father
(50 bucks an acre
Gott im Himmel I cut
down all the trees I
picked up all the stones) who

gave it to his son
(who sold it)

9.

This won't
surprise you.

My grandfather
lost the stone maul.

10.

My father (retired)
grew raspberries.
He dug in his potato patch.
He drank one glass of wine
each morning.
He was lonesome
for death.

He was lonesome for the
hot wind on his face, the smell
of horses, the distant
hum of a threshing machine,
the oilcan he carried, the weight
of a crescent wrench in his hind pocket.

He was lonesome for his absent
son and his daughters,
for his wife, for his own
brothers and sisters and
his own mother and father.

He found the stone maul
on a rockpile in the
north-west corner of what
he thought of
as his wheatfield.

He kept it (the
stone maul) on the railing
of the back porch in
a raspberry basket.

11.

I keep it
on my desk
(the stone).

Sometimes I use it
in the (hot) wind
(to hold down paper)

smelling a little of cut
grass or maybe even of
ripening wheat or of
buffalo blood hot
in the dying sun.

Sometimes I write
my poems for that

stone hammer.

The
Ledger

The Ledger

the   the ledger survived
ledger
                             because it was neither
itself   human nor useful

a. 'in bookkeeping, the book of final entry, in which a record of
   debits, credits, and all money transactions is kept.'

                                        the
                                        book
                                        of
                                        columns

page 33: James Darling

1880

Mar 22: to sawing square timber   1.44
June 21: to 1 round cedar bed   3.50
June 21: to 1 jack shingles   .50
Dec 4: to sawing mable [*sic*]   1.50   Nov 4/82 by logs   4.10

                                            (it doesn't balance)

some pages torn out (
by accident)
some pages remaining (
by accident)

page 62: Nicholas Neubecker

1893

Nov 16: to chopping 8 bags   .40
Dec 19: to chopping 880 lbs   .49
        : to elm scantling   .18

the poet: by accident
finding in the torn ledger

(IT DOESN'T BALANCE)

the green poem:

my grandfather, Henry (dead)	the ledger itself (surviving)
in his watermill (gone)	purchased in the Bruce County
on the Teeswater River,	Drug and Book Store (Price:
on the road between Formosa	$1.00 PAID, the leather cover
and Belmore,	brown. In gold:
needing a new ledger:	*THE LEDGER:*

EVERYTHING I WRITE
I SAID, IS A SEARCH
(is debit, is credit)

is a search   for some pages

                remaining

        (by accident)

the poet: finding   the column straight
in the torn ledger   the column broken

                FINDING

everything you write
my wife, my daughters, said   *the book of final entry*
is a search   for the dead   *in which a record is kept.*

b. 'a horizontal piece of timber secured to the uprights
   supporting the putlogs in a scaffolding, or the like.'

The Canada Gazette, August 17, 1854:
'Notice is hereby given that the undermentioned
lands ... in the County of Bruce, U.C., will be open
for sale to actual settlers ... The price to be Ten shil-
lings per acre ... Actual occupation to be immediate
and continuous ...'

                                      To raise a barn;

cut down a forest.

                                      To raise oats and hay;

burn the soil.

                                      To raise cattle and hogs;

kill the bear   'As to the climate of the district,
kill the mink   Father Holzer cannot praise it
kill the marten   enough. He declares that during
kill the lynx   the first nine months of his resi-
kill the fisher   dence here they had only one
kill the beaver   funeral, and that was of a man
kill the moose   84 years old.'

                         A Pristine Forest
                         A Pristine Forest

'That winter, therefore, timbers of elm and maple and pine were
cut the necessary lengths, hewed and dressed and hauled by
means of the oxen to the barn site. Cedar logs were sawn in
suitable lengths and shingles split from these blocks ...'

'TO THE SAUGEEN!'
was the cry that spread.

Henry, the elder of the two
brothers, was born in 1856,
across the river from the mill
Shaping the trees   in a log shanty measuring (as
into logs (burn   specified in *The Canada Gazette*,
the slash) into   August 17, 1854) at least six-
timbers and planks.   teen feet by eighteen.

Shaping the trees
into ledgers.
Raising the barn.

That they might sit down   to a pitcher of Formosa beer
a forest had fallen.

Shaping the trees.
Into shingles.
Into scantling.
Into tables and chairs.

Have a seat, John.   That they might sit down
Sit down, Henry.   a forest/had fallen.

page 119: John O. Miller, brickmaker in Mildmay

1888

Aug 17: to cedar shingles 12.50   Aug 17: by Brick 2500
                                       at 50¢   12.50

(I'll be damned. It balances.)

yes:no
no:yes

'... a specimen of the self-made men who have made Canada what it is, and of which no section has brought forth more or better representatives than the County of Bruce. Mr. Miller was never an office-seeker, but devoted himself strictly and energetically to the pursuit of his private business, and on his death was the owner of a very large and valuable property...'

Shaping the trees.
Pushing up daisies.

Have another glass, John.
Ja, ja. What the hell.

What's the matter, John?
My bones ache.

Take a day off, John.
No time.

A horizontal piece of timber
supporting the putlogs
in a scaffolding, or the like.

(specimens of the self-made
men who have made Canada
what is it)

The barn is still standing
(the mill, however, is gone)
sound as the day it was raised.

No time.
August 17, 1888.

No time.

Shaping the trees.
Pushing up daisies.

I'll be damned.
It balances.

c. 'one who is permanently or constantly in a place; a resident. *Obs.*'

> 'Old Gottlieb Haag was a man verging on 80 years of age. As a young man he had emigrated from Germany to America to seek his fortune and better his condition in the New World. Leaving Rotterdam in a sailing ship bound for New York, after a tedious and tempestuous voyage in which his ship was frequently blown half-way back to Europe, he finally landed on the shores of the New World. Here all his fortune lay before him.'

(Das ist doch nicht möglich!)

arrivals: the sailing ship
arrivals: the axe
arrivals: the almighty dollar

departures: the trout stream
departures: the passenger pigeon
departures: the pristine forest

arrivals: the stump fence
arrivals: the snake fence
arrivals: the stone fence

(Here all his fortune lay before him)

'As a sample of the condition of many of the early settlers on their arrival, the Clement family (who came from the Niagara frontier, crossing rivers on rafts and swimming their cattle) possessed only two axes, a hoe, ox-yoke, log-chain, a "drag" made from the crotch of a tree, and an "ox-jumper" in the way of agricultural implements; and, as things went in those days, this was considered a first-rate stock. Though very few families in this county ever suffered any inconvenience or annoyances from the aborigines, the Clements were rather roughly used by a wandering band on one occasion, who forcibly took possession of the whole roof of their shanty (which was composed chiefly of birch-bark) for the purpose of canoe-making.'

departures: the birch-bark
canoe
(ledger: a resident.
Obsolete.)

Census, 1861: County of Bruce:

2,663 horses
6,274 working oxen
19,830 cattle of all ages
29,412 sheep and swine

turnips: 848,403 bushels
wheat: 642,110 bushels
maple sugar: 170,365 lbs
cheese: 24,324 lbs

The enumerator 'got his feet frozen and another had to finish the work. Both made oath to their respective sheets and these are numbered and designated separately.'

Census, 1861: Township of Carrick:

'Indians if any'   Name: Catherine Schneider
                          Year of birth: 1841
                          Place of birth: Atlantic Ocean

                          Place of birth: Atlantis,
                          the kingdom sought
                          beyond the stone gates,
none   beyond the old home,
                          beyond the ceaseless
                          wars of the Rhine
                          Palatinate. The sought
                          continent of fortune
                          lying beyond
Gottlieb Haag's only son your father's recurring
grew up to be the first man nightmare of the (forced)
hanged for murder   march to Moscow
in the County of Bruce   (my bones ache),
                          beyond the flight
(I can't believe my eyes.) from the burning
                          fields. Beyond
having, on a wintry night, in the night of terror
a sleigh box on the road from crossing the closed
Belmore to Formosa, clubbed border. *Atlantis:*
to death his rival   the kingdom dreamed

(I can't believe my eyes.)

                    in love.

'It is well watered by the south branch of the Saugeen and a number of tributaries, which afford fine mill privileges almost in every section.'

Henry, on quiet days at the mill, on wintry days, made furniture for sale to the thriving inhabitants who intended to stay.

page 95: Mr. Peter Brick

1880

1881

Dec. 5:	to 1 bed	4.00	
"	" 6 chairs	4.50	
"	" 2 "	1.00	
"	" 1 sink	4.00	
"	" 1 dressing case	16.00	
"	" 1 side board	10.00	
"	" 1 table	4.00	Settelt [sic]

43.50   by 1 horse   43.50

Mr. Peter Brick, on the road
from Belmore to Formosa,
intending to stay ('Beer
also was plentiful and cheap.')

bought new furniture for his
new brick house and turned

the old log shanty into
a summer kitchen where   ledger: a resident.
on hot afternoons   Pushing up daisies.
he might   wait out the heat.   *Obsolete.*

d. 'the nether millstone.'

> They were draining the pond to do some
> work on the dam. Seeing a few fish at the
> floodgate, Henry sent one of his sons for a
> bucket. The boy, stepping into the water,
> catching fish with his bare hands, filled the
> bucket. Henry could hardly believe his eyes.
> But he sent the boy for a sack. And couldn't
> believe. But sent the boy for a tub, for a
> barrel.

Joe Hauck got his arm caught in the water wheel.
He screamed. But no one heard him.

He couldn't get free. The wheel was trying to
lift him up to heaven. He couldn't get free.

Joe Hauck had a good head on his shoulders, a
cap on his head. He threw his cap into the racing

water. The men unloading logs below the mill
noticed the cap; they ran on up to the millsite.

The doctor had good horses; he got there that same
day. Three men held Joe Hauck flat on a table,

right next to a saw, while the doctor patched
and sewed, ran out of thread, broke a needle.

> to
> chopping
> 8
> bags
>
> .40

you must see
the confusion again
the chaos   again
the original forest

under the turning wheel
the ripened wheat, the
razed forest, the wrung
man: the nether stone

page 117: Paul Willie

1893

by ½ Day Work	.38
'' work with team	2.00
'' 100 lbs of flour	1.85
''25 bushels lime	3.12
'' plowing potato patch	1.50
'' working at dam	2.00
Team to Mildmay	.50
by 5 cord of wood	8.00
'' beef 87 lbs at 5¢	4.35
'' hay 1,000 lbs	4.00
'' 2 hemlock logs	.75
'' 1-20 ft cedar log	.50
'' 3-16 ft cedar	.75

it doesn't balance

1854 to 1910:

to sawing Butternut
"   "   Pine
"   "   Basswood
"   "   Birch
"   "   Soft Elm
" . "   Rock Elm
"   "   Cedar
"   "   Tamarack
"   "   Maple
"   "   Beech
"   "   Black Ash
"   "   Hemlock
"   "   Cherry   it doesn't balance

The bottom of the pond was not so much mud as fish. The receding water was a wide fountain of leaping fish; Henry sent a daughter to go fetch Charlie Reinhart, Ignatz Kiefer, James Darling, Peter Brick. The neighbours began to arrive (and strangers, bearing empty sacks) from up the road to Formosa, from down the road to Belmore; the neighbours came with tubs and barrels, with a wagon box, and they clubbed at the eels that skated on the bright mud. They lunged at the leaping trout. They pounced like bullfrogs after bullfrogs. And they swam in the quick, receding flood.

the grinding stone
that does not
turn:

under the turning
stone: the nether
stone: the ledger

                    intending to stay

35

The children screamed after their leaping, swimming parents. They didn't believe their eyes. They bathed in the clean, the original mud. They flung the fish onto dry land and themselves stayed in the water: they usurped the fish. The floodgate was open, the dam no longer a dam. They rose, blue-eyed and shouting, out of the tripping, slippery mud: while the fish, their quick gills strange to the sudden air, drowned for lack of water.

The children, sitting hunched on the dam,
hearing Joe Hauck scream, were silent.

In all their lives they had never heard Joe Hauck
scream (his arm mangled: by the turning wheel).

People said Joe Hauck was never the same
after that water wheel tried lifting him

up to heaven. No matter what he did, people shook
their heads. 'He's not the same,' they said.

When his brothers went west to homestead, Joe
elected to stay at the mill. He wasn't the same.

e. 'a large flat stone, esp. one laid over a tomb.'

> *Dear Bob,*
>
> *... In regards to information about my Grandmother —*
> *your great Grandmother —Theresia Tschirhart. She was a*
> *sedate tall heavyset person, well read and could visit with*
> *the best. She did love reading and mixing with people. She*
> *was widowed three times before going west ... She passed*
> *away after trying to sit on a chair and missing it, broke her*
> *hip and was in bed for a few weeks, died and was buried in*
> *Spring Lake, Alberta. She was still very active before her*
> *fall ...*

all my love
Aunt Mary O'C

born in Alsace, she spoke
German with a French accent,
English with a German accent,

looked down on all Bavarians
for being the tree-chopping
beer drinkers they all were:

Married three Bavarians.
Buried three Bavarians.   it balances

What did most men feel
in her presence?   Terror.

What did they do about it?   Proposed.

                                       (I can't
                                       believe my eyes)

An A-1 cook.
Kept a spotless house.
She wasn't just careful,
she was tight.
Went to church more often   Men felt terror.
than was necessary.   They proposed.

Census, 1861
County of Bruce:
Deaths in 1860
(Age and Cause):

1 yr: croup
blank: born dead
5 months: fits
blank: dysentery
16 yrs: hurt
by sawmill wheel
38: 1 Deth
Inflamation

Henry's father: dead
(The doctor had good
horses)

page 88: John Mosack

in a/c Theresia ~~Kroetsch Messner~~ Hauck

Jan 19: to white ash   12.05   PAID IN FULL
Aug 24: to black ash   2.84   PAID IN FULL
Nov 10: to pine 216 ft   2.16   PAID IN FULL

Owing that woman money
was a mistake.

What do I owe you?
Seventeen dollars and five cents.
What'll you settle for?   You MUST
Seventeen dollars and five cents.   marry the terror.

Finally succumbed to the grave herself.
Spring Lake, Alberta. 1913. *Ruhe in
Frieden.*

                                    The Canadian climate:
                                    a short summer
                                    followed by a short winter
                                    followed by a short summer
                                    followed by a short winter

She was a ringtailed snorter   (you must marry
just the same.   the terror)

1913
1829
———
  84

Cause of death: She lies buried to the east
                                  of the church in Spring Lake,
went to sit down   Alberta. She was visiting in
and missed the chair   Heisler, Alberta, at the time
                                  of her death: Heisler was so
                                  new it didn't have a graveyard:

                                  DEATH PROHIBITED
Verdammt!   ON THESE PREMISES

What do I owe you?

                                  O bury me not
                                  on the lone prairie.

WHAT DO I OWE YOU?
WHAT DO I OWE YOU?

Where the coyotes howl
and the wind blows free.

Even by-God dead
washed
dressed
laid out   her desire to be interred
she indicated   in the plot of Ontario earth
(she was a ringttailed   next to the ledger that
snorter just the same)   covered her first husband:

zum andenken von

LORENZ KROETSCH

gestorben den
13th Feb 1860
alt 38 Jahre

Ruhe nun im sanften schlummer   inflammation
In der erde kühlem schoos   of
Hier entwichen allem kummer   the
Ist der friede nun dein loos   lungs:
Noch umringen wir dein grab   coughed
Schauen wehmuts voll hinab   gagged
Doch zur ruhe gehn auch wir   choked
Gott sei dank wir folgen dir.   died.

Requiescat in Pace

No one would pay the shot.
The CPR wouldn't do it   An Alberta grave
for love.   is a cold, cold grave.

40

f. 'a book that lies permanently in some place.'

> A man that lies permanently in some place.
> A woman that lies permanently in some place.
> A resident. *Obsolete.*
> The book of final entry.

The book
of columns.
The book that lies
permanently.

> The timber supporting the putlogs
> in a scaffolding:

e.g., the poem   in the chaos

> in the dark night
> in the beautiful forest

'With no effort or pretension to literary merit, the object will be rather to present a plain statement of facts of general interest which bear upon the past growth and development of this wonderfully prosperous section of the Province, in such manner as to render future comparisons more easy, and offer to the rising generation an incentive to emulation in the examples of the pioneers, whose self-reliant industry and progressive enterprise have conquered the primeval forests, and left in their stead, as a heritage to posterity, a country teeming with substantial comforts and material wealth, and reflecting in its every feature the indomitable spirit and true manliness of a noble race, whose lives and deeds will shine while the communities they have founded shall continue to exist.'

Gottlieb Haag's only son	(with no effort
(for the first murder	
in the County of Bruce)	or pretension
Hanged.	to literary merit)

'Caoutchouc usually mowed down three or four spellers. When it didn't, such words as gubernatorial or phthisicky or threnody would do the trick.'

Henry. How do you spell maple?　　　m-a-b-l-e

Henry. How do you spell balance?　　b-a-l-l-o-n-s

Henry. How do you spell Henry?　　　H-e-n-e-r-y

Threnody:
a song
of lamentation.

the ledger itself
survives

page 69: Edward McGue　　　　intending to stay

1886

to hemlock rafters　　　5.01
to cedar shakes　　　　18.75　the roof over his head

1887

to hemlock fencing　　　5.10
to 1 plow　　　　　　　9.15　the sod beneath his boots

the ledger stone
the nether stone

either would do
the lasting trick

the stone singing
song on the stone

Robert Nickel   the ledger itself
John Molloy
Jacob Sagmiller   surviving
PAID IN FULL
Luke Steigler   beyond the last felling
Pat Mahoney   beyond the last tree felled
George Straus   the last turn of the wheel
PAID IN FULL   the last coin worn and gone
Fleming Ballogh   from the last pocket
Michel Kirby   worn
Robert Curl
PAID IN FULL   and gone
John Elder   beyond the last turned page
Michael Laporte   beyond the last
Richard McDaniel
PAID IN FULL   entry
Christian Kirschmer
Henry Busby
William Trench
PAID IN FULL
Joseph Hall
Peter Shoemaker
David Rush
PAID IN FULL

'They had to cut down three trees in order to
bury the first man dead in Formosa.'

Some people go to heaven.   Cut to the rock
Some people write poems.   the rock rose up.
Some people go west   Tombstones are hard
to homestead.   to kill.

REST IN PEACE
You Must Marry the Terror

Seed

Catalogue

Seed Catalogue

1.

No. 176 – *Copenhagen Market Cabbage:* 'This *new introduction,
strictly speaking,* is in every respect a *thoroughbred,* a *cabbage* of
highest pedigree, and is *creating considerable flurry* among *pro-
fessional gardeners* all *over the world.'*

We took the storm windows/off
the south side of the house
and put them on the hotbed.
Then it was spring. Or, no:
then winter was ending.

> 'I wish to say we had lovely success
> this summer with the seed purchased
> of you. We had the finest Sweet
> Corn in the country, and Cabbage
> were dandy.'
>   – W.W. Lyon, South Junction, Man.

> My mother said:
> Did you wash your ears?
> You could grow cabbages
> in those ears.

Winter was ending.
This is what happened:
we were harrowing the garden.
You've got to understand this:
I was sitting on the horse.
The horse was standing still.
I fell off.

The hired man laughed: how
in hell did you manage to
fall off a horse that was
standing still?

        Bring me the radish seeds,
        my mother whispered.

Into the dark of January
the seed catalogue bloomed

a winter proposition, if
spring should come, then,

with illustrations:

No. 25 — *McKenzie's Improved Golden Wax Bean:* 'THE MOST
PRIZED OF ALL BEANS. *Virtue* is its own reward. We have had
many expressions from *keen discriminating gardeners extolling
our seed* and *this variety.'*

        Beans, beans,
        the musical fruit;
        the more you eat,
        the more you virtue.

My mother was marking the first row
with a piece of binder twine, stretched
between two pegs.

The hired man laughed: just
about planted the little bugger.
Cover him up and see what grows.

My father didn't laugh. He was puzzled
by any garden that was smaller than a
quarter-section of wheat and summerfallow.

the home place: N.E. 17-42-16-W4th Meridian.

the home place: one and a half miles west of Heisler, Alberta,
                    on the correction line road
                    and three miles south.

No trees
around the house.
Only the wind.
Only the January snow.
Only the summer sun.
The home place:
a terrible symmetry.

How do you grow a gardener?

        Telephone Peas
        Garden Gem Carrots
        Early Snowcap Cauliflower
        Perfection Globe Onions
        Hubbard Squash
        Early Ohio Potatoes

This is what happened — at my mother's wake. This
is a fact — the World Series was in progress. The
Cincinnati Reds were playing the Detroit Tigers.
It was raining. The road to the graveyard was barely
passable. The horse was standing still. Bring me
the radish seeds, my mother whispered.

2.

My father was mad at the badger: the badger was digging holes in the potato patch, threatening man and beast with broken limbs (I quote). My father took the double-barrelled shotgun out into the potato patch and waited.

Every time the badger stood up, it looked like a little man, come out of the ground. Why, my father asked himself — Why would so fine a fellow live under the ground? Just for the cool of roots? The solace of dark tunnels? The blood of gophers?

My father couldn't shoot the badger. He uncocked the shotgun, came back to the house in time for breakfast. The badger dug another hole. My father got mad again. They carried on like that all summer.

> *Love is an amplification*
> *by doing/ over and over.*
>
> *Love is a standing up*
> *to the loaded gun.*
>
> *Love is a burrowing.*

One morning my father actually shot at the badger. He killed a magpie that was pecking away at a horse turd about fifty feet beyond and to the right of the spot where the badger had been standing.

A week later my father told the story again. In that version he intended to hit the magpie. Magpies, he explained, are a nuisance. They eat robins' eggs. They're harder to kill than snakes, jumping around the way they do, nothing but feathers.

Just call me sure-shot,
my father added.

3.

No. 1248 — *Hubbard Squash:* 'As *mankind* seems to have a
particular fondness for squash, *Nature* appears to have *especially*
provided this *matchless* variety of *superlative flavor.*'

> *Love is a leaping up*
> *and down.*
>
> *Love*
> *is a beak in the warm flesh.*

'As a cooker, it heads the list for warted squash. The
vines are of strong running growth; the fruits are large,
olive shaped, of a deep rich green color, the rind is
smooth ...'

But how do you grow a lover?

This is the God's own truth:
playing dirty is a mortal sin
the priest told us, you'll go to hell
and burn forever (with illustrations) —

it was our second day of catechism
— Germaine and I went home that
afternoon   if it's that bad, we
said to each other   we realized
we better quit   we realized

let's do it just one last time
and quit.

This is the God's own truth:
catechism, they called it,
the boys had to sit in the pews
on the right, the girls on the left.
Souls were like underwear that you
wore inside. If boys and girls sat
together —

Adam and Eve got caught
playing dirty.

This is the truth.
We climbed up into a granary
full of wheat   to the gunny sacks
the binder twine was shipped in —

we spread the paper from the sacks
smooth sheets   on the soft wheat
Germaine and I   we were like/one

we had discovered, don't ask me
how, where — but when the priest said
playing dirty we knew — well —

he had named it   he had named
our world   out of existence
(the horse   was standing still)

— This is my first confession. Bless me father I played
   dirty so long, just the other day, up in the granary
   there by the car shed — up there on the Brantford Binder
   Twine gunny sacks and the sheets of paper — Germaine
   with her dress up and her bloomers down —

— Son. For penance, keep your peter in your pants
   for the next thirteen years.

But how —

          Adam and Eve and Pinch-Me
          went down to the river to swim —
          Adam and Eve got drownded.

But how do you grow a lover?

          We decided we could do it
          just one last time.

4.

It arrived in winter, the seed catalogue, on a January
day. It came into town on the afternoon train.

Mary Hauck, when she came west from Bruce County, Ontario,
arrived in town on a January day. She brought along
her hope chest.

She was cooking in the Heisler Hotel. The Heisler Hotel
burned down on the night of June 21, 1919. Everything
in between: lost. Everything: an absence

of satin sheets
of embroidered pillow cases
of tea towels and English china
of silver serving spoons.

How do you grow a prairie town?

                    The gopher was the model.
                    Stand up straight:
                    telephone poles
                    grain elevators
                    church steeples.
                    Vanish, suddenly: the
                    gopher was the model.

How do you grow a past/
to live in

the absence of silkworms
the absence of clay and wattles (whatever the hell
                they are)
the absence of Lord Nelson
the absence of kings and queens
the absence of a bottle opener, and me with a vicious
                attack of the 26-ounce flu
the absence of both Sartre and Heidegger
the absence of pyramids
the absence of lions
the absence of lutes, violas and xylophones
the absence of a condom dispenser in the Lethbridge Hotel and
                me about to screw an old Blood whore. I was
                in love.
the absence of the Parthenon, not to mention the Cathédrale de
                Chartres
the absence of psychiatrists
the absence of sailing ships
the absence of books, journals, daily newspapers and everything
                else but the *Free Press Prairie Farmer* and *The
                Western Producer*
the absence of gallows (with apologies to Louis Riel)
the absence of goldsmiths
the absence of the girl who said that if the Edmonton Eskimos
                won the Grey Cup she'd let me kiss her
                nipples in the foyer of the Palliser Hotel. I
                don't know where she got to.
the absence of Heraclitus
the absence of the Seine, the Rhine, the Danube, the Tiber and
                the Thames. Shit, the Battle River ran dry
                one fall. The Strauss boy could piss across it.
                He could piss higher on a barn wall than any
                of us. He could piss right clean over the
                principal's new car.
the absence of ballet and opera
the absence of Aeneas

How do you grow a prairie town?

Rebuild the hotel when it burns down. Bigger. Fill it
full of a lot of A-1 Hard Northern Bullshitters.

— You ever hear the one about the woman who buried
  her husband with his ass sticking out of the ground
  so that every time she happened to walk by she could
  give it a swift kick?

— Yeh, I heard it.

5.

I planted some melons, just to see what would
happen. Gophers ate everything.

                              I applied to the Government.
                              I wanted to become a postman,
                              to deliver real words
                              to real people.

                              There was no one to receive
                              my application.

I don't give a damn if I do die do die do die do die do die
do die do die do die do die do die do die do die do die do
die do die do die do die do die do die do die do die do die
do

6.

No. 339 — *McKenzie's Pedigreed Early Snowcap Cauliflower:* 'Of the many *varieties* of *vegetables* in *existence, Cauliflower* is *unquestionably* one of the *greatest inheritances* of the *present generation, particularly Western Canadians.* There is *no place* in the *world* where *better cauliflowers* can be *grown* than right here in the *West.* The *finest specimens* we have *ever seen,* larger and of *better quality,* are *annually grown* here on our *prairies.* Being *particularly* a *high altitude plant* it *thrives* to a *point* of *perfection* here, *seldom seen* in *warmer climes.'*

But how do you grow a poet?

Start: with an invocation
invoke —

His muse is
his muse/if
memory is

and you have
no memory then
no meditation
no song (shit
we're up against it)

how about that girl
you felt up in the
school barn or that
girl you necked with
out by Hastings' slough
and ran out of gas with
and nearly froze to
death with/ or that
girl in the skating
rink shack who had on
so much underwear you
didn't have enough
prick to get past her/
CCM skates

Once upon a time in the village of Heisler —

— Hey, wait a minute.
That's a story.

How do you grow a poet?

For appetite: cod-liver
oil.
For bronchitis: mustard
plasters.
For pallor and failure to fill
the woodbox: sulphur
& molasses.
For self-abuse: ten Our
Fathers & ten Hail Marys.
For regular bowels: Sunny Boy
Cereal.

How do you grow a poet?

'It's a pleasure to advise that I
won the First Prize at the Calgary
Horticultural Show... This is my
first attempt. I used your seeds.'

Son, this is a crowbar.
This is a willow fencepost.
This is a sledge.
This is a roll of barbed wire.
This is a bag of staples.
This is a claw hammer.

We give form to this land by running
a series of posts and three strands
of barbed wire around a quarter-section.

First off I want you to take that
crowbar and drive 1,156 holes
in that gumbo.
And the next time you want to
write a poem
we'll start the haying.

How do you grow a poet?

This is a prairie road.
This road is the shortest distance
between nowhere and nowhere.
This road is a poem.

Just two miles up the road
you'll find a porcupine
dead in the ditch. It was
trying to cross the road.

As for the poet himself
we can find no record
of his having traversed
the land/in either direction

no trace of his coming
or going/only a scarred
page, a spoor of wording
a reduction to mere black

and white/a pile of rabbit
turds that tells us
all spring long
where the track was

poet ... say uncle.

How?

Rudy Wiebe: 'You must lay great black steel lines of
fiction, break up that space with huge design and, like
the fiction of the Russian steppes, build a giant
artifact. No song can do that ...'

February 14, 1976. Rudy, you
took us there: to the Oldman River
Lorna & Byrna, Ralph & Steve and me
you showed us where
the Bloods surprised the Crees
in the next coulee/surprised
them to death. And after
you showed us Rilke's word
Lebensgliedes.

Rudy: Nature thou art.

7.

Brome Grass (Bromus Inermis): 'No amount of cold will kill it. It *withstands* the summer suns. Water may stand on it for several weeks without apparent injury. The roots push through the soil, throwing up new plants continually. It *starts quicker* than other grasses in the spring. *Remains green* longer in the fall. *Flourishes under absolute neglect.'*

The end of winter:
seeding/time.

*How do you grow
a poet?*

(a)

I was drinking with Al Purdy. We went round and round
in the restaurant on top of the Chateau Lacombe. We
were the turning center in the still world, the winter
of Edmonton was hardly enough to cool our out-sights.

The waitress asked us to leave. She was rather insistent;
we were bad for business, shouting poems at the paying
customers. Twice, Purdy galloped a Cariboo horse
right straight through the dining area.

Now that's what I call
a piss-up.

                'No song can do that.'

(b)
No. 2362 – *Imperialis Morn-*
ing Glory: 'This is the won-
derful *Japanese Morning*
Glory, celebrated the world
over for its *wondrous beauty*
of both flowers and foliage.'

Sunday, January 12, 1975. This evening after
rereading *The Double Hook*: looking at Japanese prints.
Not at actors. Not at courtesans. Rather: Hiroshige's
series, *Fifty-Three Stations on the Tokaido.*

From the *Tokaido* series: 'Shono-Haku-u.' The
bare-assed travellers, caught in a sudden shower.
Men and trees, bending. How it is in a rain shower/
that you didn't see coming. And couldn't have avoided/
even if you had.

> The double hook:
> the home place.
>
> The stations of the way:
> the other garden
>
> *Flourishes.*
> *Under absolute neglect.*

(c)

Jim Bacque said (I was waiting for a plane,
after a reading; Terminal 2, Toronto) — he said,
You've got to deliver the pain to some woman,
don't you?

— Hey, Lady.
   You at the end of the bar.
   I wanna tell you something.

— Yuh?

— Pete Knight — of Crossfield,
   Alberta. Bronc-Busting Champion
   of the World. You ever hear of
   Pete Knight, the King of All
   Cowboys, Bronc-Busting Champion
   of the World?

— Huh-uh.

— You know what I mean? King
   of *All* Cowboys ... Got
   killed — by a horse.
   He fell off.

— You some kind of nut
   or something?

8.

We silence words
by writing them down.

(a) [yes, his first bequest]

To my son Frederick my carpenter tools.

It was his first bequest. First,
a man must build.

Those horse-barns around Heisler —
those perfectly designed barns
with the rounded roofs — only Freddie
knew how to build them. He mapped
the parklands with perfect horse-barns.

> I remember my Uncle Freddie.
> (The farmers no longer
> use horses.)
>
> Back in the 30s, I remember
> he didn't have enough money
> to buy a pound of coffee.
>
> Every morning at breakfast
> he drank a cup of hot water
> with cream and sugar in it.
>
> Why, I asked him one morning —
> I wasn't all that old — why
> do you do that? I asked him.
>
> Jesus Christ, he said. He was
> a gentle man, really. Don't you
> understand *anything*?

9.

The danger of merely living.

a shell/exploding
in the black sky: a
strange planting

a bomb/exploding
in the earth: a
strange

man/falling
on the city.
Killed him dead.

It was a strange
planting.

the absence of my cousin who was shot down while bombing
the city that was his maternal great-grandmother's
birthplace. He was the navigator. He guided himself
to that fatal occasion:

> — a city he had
>   forgotten
> — a woman he had
>   forgotten

He intended merely to release a cargo of bombs on a
target and depart. The exploding shell was:

a) an intrusion on a design that was not his, or

b) an occurrence which he had in fact, unintentionally,
    himself designed, or

c) it is essential that we understand this matter
    because:

He was the first descendant of that family to return
to the Old Country. He took with him: a cargo of bombs.

> Anna Weller: *Geboren* Cologne, 1849.
> Kenneth MacDonald: Died Cologne, 1943.

> A terrible symmetry.

A strange muse: forgetfulness. Feeding her far children
to ancestral guns, blasting them out of the sky, smack/
into the earth. Oh, she was the mothering sort. Blood/
on her green thumb.

10.

After the bomb/blossoms   *Poet, teach us*
After the city/falls   *to love our dying.*
After the rider/falls
(the horse   *West is a winter place.*
standing still)   *The palimpsest of prairie*

                                 under the quick erasure
                                 of snow, invites a flight.

How/do you grow a garden?

(a)

        No. 3060 — *Spencer Sweet Pea:*
        Pkt. $.10; oz. $.25;
        quarter lb. $.75; half lb. $1.25.

Your sweet peas
climbing the staked
chicken wire,
climbing the stretched
binder twine by
the front porch

taught me the smell
of morning, the grace
of your tired
hands, the strength
of a noon sun, the
colour of prairie grass

taught me the smell
of my sweating armpits.

(b)

How do you a garden grow?
How do you grow a garden?

'Dear Sir,
        The longest brome grass I remember seeing was
one night in Brooks. We were on our way up to the Calgary
Stampede, and reached Brooks about 11 pm, perhaps earlier
because there was still a movie on the drive-in screen.
We unloaded Cindy, and I remember tying her up to the truck
box and the brome grass was up to her hips. We laid down
in the back of the truck – on some grass I pulled by hand –
and slept for about three hours, then drove into Calgary.
                                                    Amie'

(c)

No trees
around the house,
only the wind.
Only the January snow.
Only the summer sun.

Adam and Eve got drownded –
Who was left?

How I
Joined
The Seal
Herd

How I Joined the Seal Herd

I swear it was not   the hearing
itself   I first refused
it was   the sight of my ears

in the mirror: the sight
of my ears   was the first
clue: my head did not please me

the seals so loud   I could hardly
accept the message: she wanted
no other going/than to be gone   the

neat bed itself   strange in the
mirror, she   kneeling across the bed
to close the window: maybe

I have this wrong: but only then
I saw   my ears/the difference
she wanted to go   I heard

a loud snort   a throaty grunt:
it was the breeding season   the tide
low, the wind still: they'd be wary

I knew, the seals   lying together
in the hot sun   maybe 300 seals
I counted   slipping off my shoes

the effect was immediate   I learned
to let my body give   it was not I
who controlled the rocks   I learned

curling my stockinged toes   to the
granite cracks and edges: maybe
I have this wrong   but I knew

in the first instant   of my courage
I must undo my very standing/crawl
on the wet rocks, the sand   not

standing   ease down on my belly:
it was strange at first   looking up
at the world: but I arched my back

I turned my head and paused   what
was I doing there on the beach/   wait
the luminous eyes of a young   seal cow:

I, the lone bull seal   bravely
guarding the rookery   alone
holding together a going world/   but

frankly, I wanted to get laid   she was
maybe five feet tall (long)   the cow:
I could see   she didn't like my clothes/

moving carefully   avoiding any fuss
I unbuttoned, I unzipped   squirmed
out of my shorts, my socks   it was, yes

quite frankly   love at first sight/
flicking, with my left hand   some sand
over my back   for an instant

I thought of my wallet   my driver's
license, my credit cards: she had dark
fur on her belly   a delicate nose:

she went towards the water   looking
back over her shoulder/   the water
looking iceberg cold   I wasn't quite ready

she was rushing me: men in their forties
I shouted after her   are awfully good
in bed (on a sandbank   I corrected myself)

alone   I lay in the sand, I lay
watching   the slow coming of each wave
to the merciful shore   I humped

down to the water's curl   I, yes
without thinking,   *without thinking,* I
dove   my ears shrank

back   to my badly designed skull: under
the water: opening my eyes   I saw
the school of herring   SNAP

I had one in my teeth   I surfaced
hungry   I let myself float head up
on the lifting waves   I hauled out

I lolled: the cow that nudged me
awake: she might have been just plain
curious   my ear-flaps, my exterior testicles/

that crossed my mind   or slightly perverse
but the sun had warmed me again   we were both
well   I was still a man, I had to talk:

my nights are all bloody   I whispered
god, I am lonely   as a lover/my
naked body swims   in the leak of light

death has a breath too   it smells
of bedclothes   it smells of locked
windows   my nights are all drenched/

my body/I   saw she had no idea
well/that was nicer, even   than the
moist hunger   in her eyes

I brushed   at my grey beard/
my flipper   trying to make the hairs
look like   vibrissae (I believe is the word)

I wasn't quite ready when   the bull hit me
I whirled   caught his neck
in my teeth   roared at the sonofabitch

slammed my head   against his nose:
he was gone/   the cow had noticed
everything   I could tell/she would

dance now/first   dance, slapping
the rising tide   to a quick froth:
she/I   rolling the waves themselves

back to the sea   I dared beyond the
last limit   of whatever I thought
I was   where, exactly, I asked, is —

my only question   and when she gave
herself/took   me out of the seen land
this, for the gone world   I sang:

America was a good lay   she nearly
fucked me to death, wow   but this
I'm a new man   (mammal, I corrected

myself) here   and yet I was going
too far   too far past everything
dispersed past   everything here/gone

dear, I whispered   (words again,
words)   I wanted to say/I am
writing   this poem   with my life

I whispered,   I hope (the rising
tide had lifted my socks   had swum
them to where   I might reach)

dear, I whispered   I hope my children
(ours, I corrected myself)   their ears perfect
will look   exactly like both of us.

The Sad
Phoenician

and even if it's true, that my women all have new lovers,
     then laugh, go ahead
but don't expect me to cry
and believe you me I have a few tricks up my sleeve myself
but I'm honest, I'm nothing if not honest; a friend of mine
     in Moose Jaw who shall remain anonymous tells me he met
     the girl from Swift Current who scorned my offer of sex
     in a tree house; a bird in the hand, he said, joking,
     of course
and flapped his arms
but she didn't speak, she told him nothing, at least not a
     particular of her need for me
and I didn't let on that I got the message
but I recognized in an instant that I'd been the cause of
     her sweating, her shortness of breath
and true, I'd be off like a shot to see her
but the woman in Montreal is not so evasive, not so given
     to outright lies, deceptions
and when she gets the letter I wrote last night, she'll say
but darling, I was following a fire truck
and quite by accident found the divine, ha, flicker
but if I don't even bother to mail the letter she'll learn
     what it feels like to be ignored
and the girl from Swift Current, the woman, can go climb a
     tree, I'm human too, you know, no slur intended

but frankly
and I don't think a little frankness would kill any of us,
I had my peek into the abyss, my brush with the verities,
such as they are, my astounding fall from innocence, you
better believe it
but I'm all right, don't feel you should worry, the
responsibility is mine, I can take care of myself
and the next time you feel like deceiving someone, why not
try yourself
but I have my work to sustain me, my poetry, the satisfaction
of a job well done
and even if I don't get the recognition I deserve, so what,
who cares
but time will tell: I keep thinking of Melville, who nearly
went mad, possibly did, out of sheer neglect
and Van Gogh; I guess you've heard that one, ha
but the woman from Swift Current who didn't have the decency
to say goodby, she'll get her just reward; there's a
reckoning in this world, you bet you me

and   virtue will out; I have my integrity; I know my own
      worth
but   I do have feelings, just because I'm a poet doesn't mean
      I have no feelings of my own, poets are human; I am, you
      might say, a kind of Phoenician, with reference, that is,
      to my trading in language, even in, to stretch a point,
      ha, my being at sea
and   the Phoenicians gave us the whole works
but   what does that matter to a world that ignores them, the
      Greeks got all the credit of course, because they stole
      the alphabet
and   the girl from Swift Current, she more or less took
      everything
but   the kitchen sink, claiming all my books, my records,
      my prints; she moved in with that photographer from
      Saskatoon, the one who takes those sterling pictures
      of the wind
and   I should sue
but   she follows large flocks of birds, I hear, calling my
      name
and   pleading

but   why she developed a thing for adverbs, that's too rich
        for my blood, I want to tell you

and shortly she'll repent, *ha*

but   I do respect her privacy

and as for the one who runs after doorknobs now: the world
        is not so round as she would have it, nor the door always
        hung to swing open

but   I keep my trap shut, I was dealt a tough mitt

and any port in a storm they say: the dreamer, himself:
        lurching, leaping, flying; o to be mere gerund; no past,
        no future: what do you do in life: I ing

but   the door, cracked, opened; the lover who would, did; the
        night knelt into morning

and is it not true that black is the absence of deceit

but   do not ask

and asking, do not wait for the sun to bring light nor for
        the rain to fall, nor for women to remember, nor for
        interest to gather capital, nor for dictators to open
        gates, nor for laughter to win elections, nor for grey
        hair to darken, except in the earth

but   that's okay, we study

and what we do not learn is how everything is: the exact
        color of midnight varies, actually; the gin is not always,
        quite, insufficient; once a year a rubber breaks and we
        learn to count; the sun, in Tuktoyaktuk, disappears
        entirely for what should have been days

but   I'm all right now, don't feel you should worry

and   that brings to mind, if I might say so, my own sterling
insights into the pseudonymous works of poor dear
Kierkegaard, nagging his way into heaven, wiping his ass
on the end of the world; he was no slouch with women,
God knows

but   love hurt him; don't I know how he felt; just ask me

and   why not tell the truth: I, The Sad Phoenician of Love,
slighted by the woman from — Nanaimo, I think it was,
yes, Nanaimo — she who lives in a submarine

but   I gave her tat for tit

and   that reminds me, I owe myself a letter too, a gentle
apology for sins of omission, ha, emission, well, let
the chips fall

but   I was only joking when I suggested, we could go down
together, hoo

and   a rose by any other name

but   let us call her A; she shall henceforth be referred to
as A; right, eh

and   henceforth, everlastingly, A she shall be

but I can see where some people might prefer just plain
outright lies, as did Ms. R, the woman in Montreal,
she who follows fires to firemen, who fell in love with
a four-stroke engine

and frankly, I'd be the last person on earth to criticize
an interest in the mechanical world

but there is nature, you know, there is such a thing as
nature

and I don't think anyone has ever been the worse for — well,
I was going to say, a call of nature — I mean, a visit
to nature

but there is also artifice, of course, not to be confused
with deception; i.e., on the one hand, a) the foot; on
the other hand, b) the shoe

and the shoes I'm wearing this morning, it just so happens,
are a shade tight across the arch; not too tight, mind
you

but tight enough to be called tight; that is, the shoe on my
right foot is a shade too tight, the shoe on my left foot
fits like a glove

and naturally I think of the foot as we refer to foot in
the line of poetry; in the traditional line, that is

but the poem must resist the poet, always, I can't help
thinking

and the woman in Nanaimo, she who lives in a submarine:
the salmon creak at her window, the water her sky;
x marks the known, the spot where she was

but isn't

82

and I'm sick of being galley slave to a penny's worth of
     words, sick of it; yes, I'm perfectly fine, except for
     a slight touch of mental prostration, dyspepsia, dropsy,
     consumption, bronchitis, the bleeding piles
but they only hurt when I laugh, ha; despondency, spitting
     of blood, catarrh, a rare combination of dysentery
and constipation, locomotor ataxis, hiccups, spermatorrhea,
     a hacking cough
but I don't smoke, I'm too nervous
and night sweats that would kill an ox, I can wring out my
     sheets in the morning; sheets, ha, pun
but the doctor gives me a clean bill of health, eat less,
     he says, drink lots of water, write to your local printer,
     sleep on a hard bed
and keep your hands on top of the quilt

but   there's no satisfying women, so why try; the hero; yes,
       right, by all means, dead on: a quest for a woman who
       might be satisfied, the holy grail nothing, poor old
       Who?him gets it into his brief case, he puts out to sea,
       so to speak, for himself
and   a bird in the hand, he soon discovers, two in ambush,
       both of them friends, pirating an edition, ha
but   if the fish complain of water
and   when the goat wears a halo, then I too shall be
       faithful, believe me; a man faithful, a woman satisfied
but   if I am not mistaken, night follows day, cows eat grass

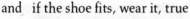

and if the shoe fits, wear it, true

but the poet must resist the poem, if you know what I mean:
take, for instance, the woman from Swift Current, she
who now loves adverbs

and I hope she's happy, I'm happy myself

but you try sitting in this room, sit on your butt, ho,
fingers raised like talons

and say out loud, to yourself, to the window if you prefer:
I'm in love

but I'm over it now, I seldom think of her as anything more
than a good, if you'll pardon my saying so, piece

and that was rather nice, I can honestly say I miss that

but there's all as well as iota, after as well as before,
you know; scratch as well as itch, bite as well as
bait, ruin as well as rut, apollonian as well as crazy
out of your head

and I don't blame them for hiking over the hills after a
pack of illusions, I'm not a vindictive man

but   let's pretend that only women suffer

and   that brings to mind a paragon; I mean, she, down there in upstate New York, she who runs after doorknobs

but   thimbles; why thimbles; doorknobs I can see, rocking chairs, trundle beds, dry sinks, fly swatters

and   I might add that more than one woman has said of me, he is, for all his distance, his peccadilloes, his passing infidelities, his inability to boil water, really, the best intentioned of men

but   stop putting words in my mouth, she said, ha

and   yet we do, after all, reason from analogy: is it not a commonplace, for instance, to compare the undulating hills of whatever distant horizon to the breasts of a nearby woman, or vice versa

but   no, you will say, to paragon is elsewhere, let hic be ille

and   yet *The Song of Solomon*, taking the first text that comes to hand, is chockful of just such analogies, heap of wheat: belly; flock of sheep: teeth

but   the woman in Nanaimo, she who lives in a submarine, has, I am told by reliable sources, become enamoured; she is hung up on clams, though why is a mystery to me, I haven't the foggiest

and   the theory itself fails, the doctrine of, I forget what;
not the chain of being, Christ knows, I've tried that
one on

but   I can love, even the black holes, even the gaited sun,
the galloping night, the earthworm riding the silver
grass

and   the bursting guts of this old cinder

but   I'm down today, I'm *don't*

and   take it from me, I am dwarf to her needments, I lug
them, after, uphill

but   every cloud has

and   only the surge of blood commends the folly, the belly's
worth, the rotund making of round, the reason why monks
look hollow, the wind has full cheeks, blow, thou

but   I've sworn off myself

and   a stiff has no conscience

but I'll tell you something, I'll let you in on a secret
and why the ladies haven't guessed my longing, that
buffaloes me
but here goes: throw salt over your left shoulder, avoid
cracks, ha, walk away from rather than toward, spell
pig backwards
and say funny
but I mean: all things being equal, fight fire with fire
and might not the flame be me, get it; he is a manifestation
of I
but haven't we met
and might I not be the doorknob too, for whatever earthly
reason, the trundle bed, the dial of her phone
but the woman from Swift Current, putting on airs, avoiding
the climb, she knew avoidance
and there are adverbs, you may remember, of manner, of place,
of time; it is possible to be decently alive
but here
and now, of course, it isn't fashionable, it isn't done
but I, The Sad Phoenician of Love, surveying the stars, the
old singer, his foot in his mouth, have a right to my
opinions

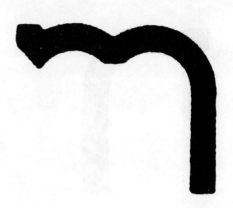

and   I still think a tree house would have solved all my
problems, well, half my problems; peek up her skirt
once in a while, sure

but   pull up the ladder or push it away; your kick at the
cat, Ludwig

and   she did say something about my being for the birds

but   of course, trust my luck, I wasn't listening, I was
hardly conscious, I was, you might say, in seventh
heaven, I might have been

and   further, kissing the backs of her knees, climbing,
her cheeky ass umbrella, as I climbed, against
disaster, Mr. Ladderman, please, she would have said

but   I'm nothing if not honest

and   I wouldn't, except, of course, to please her, raise
even my voice

but   it was she who resisted; she, wronged by refusing;
life is what we make it they say; maybe even stones have
discourse, perhaps there is a music of the spheres,
heard on quiet nights, far from water

and   maybe the fireman only climbs to kiss the flame

but even if it's true, that my women all have new lovers,
offer no pity, remember, the worm turns
and could it not be argued, the grease gets the squeaking
wheel, the bridegroom the bride, the knot gets all or
nun, ha, the sea sits firmly on top of land
but I live by a kind of resistance
and that explains why I was not there when she hollered
uncle, the huntress, she with her glasses strung to
her neck, the guide concealed in her canvas purse, a
Franklin stove for a mouth, a rocker her hat or hair,
two vinegar bottles under her blouse, behind her a
round oak table
but the eye is a liar, the sun does not set
and any rogue of the first water would know how to wait,
time flies, there are other fish in the ocean
but enough: let one be the square root of one
and lonely is only lonely, it has no other name like
hand or hope or trust, or pissing against the wind,
it has no habit of upside-down, it slams no doors,
it does not fly south in autumn
but I love you

and if the ladder isn't there when I step off, then he
     who photographs the wind may find me in the picture,
     yes
but give a guy a chance, would you
and if oops is the right name for accident, then I have
     come full circle
but grief has its o too, the ice cream fallen from the
     cone, the child learning, the orifice of love, open
and happy the happy oo, as in rue; surprise at the ancient
     pleasure
but ouch my ass is dragging
and that means the end can't be far away, ha; well, all
     right, I confess: the woman in Montreal, she took
     up with an old flame
but you could have warned me, I told her; oh, she said
and I, the anarchist who needed order, wearing a dandelion
     at my throat

but Miss Reading would look at the fire, not at the light;
     here's pie on your plate, compose yourself, trala trala
and I guessed it: the night to her was everything; she
     could not read it by day, she who bought books
but only for the torn page: the burning was her alphabet
and she hurried, sometimes she had not a minute to spare,
     she praised me, **wantonly**
but the mouth gives entrance to exit, kissy-boo

and meaning: even in that she found meaning, if not a
      mime
but I, The Sad Phoenician of Love, dyeing the world red,
      dyed laughing, ha, lost everything, lost home; I,.
      homing
and lost: while she, the children off to school, on the
      Q.T. whispered: stay away from sunsets, poet, sleep
      with a window open, on cloudy days take Vitamin C,
      never trust water
but track the snail, trick the murex down to red, the
      last Tyrian purple, worship
and worship darkly, too; the purple fish, into the round
      ship, raise; a quaint devouring, this or then
but nothing matters, I told her; true, she said, so much,
      so what, you can't get blood from a turnip
and that's that, I suppose

but somewhere today your body is waiting, we rely on the
    flesh; love is only the consequence, not the cause. Or
    vice versa. How green, actually, green is.

And when the dog says grrr, then we are going from bad to
    burn. Colder than hell, the prairie this morning,
    frost on the growing grass. The tree house wearing
    its leafy parka. Yuk.

But where shall I say you have gone? she said. The poet
    blew his nose. It's not green, he answered.

And the submarine too. Inexplicable. Except for the
    prevalence of same. Even in dark places. See Henry,
    I beg your pardon, Henri.

But eat your oysters while you are. Horny contains: a
    reminding. A regretting. A regressing. A returning.
    A pretending. A simpering. A forswearing. A
    slithering. A sundering.

And the usual remonstrance, of course, double or nothing,
    get hold of yourself

but no remedy

and feeding the beast of her humor, I rampage into my
own grave, 'sblood

but still we ask, does the lion dream the sleeper or the
sleeper the lion

and s.o.s. says sink or swim; down is out; the cardinal,
in season only, wears red

but the plural of would is not, if you see what I mean;
don't turpentine the dog for chasing a falling star;
you will, won't you, feed no bears; they lick each
other's thighs, the lovers

and a slip of the tongue is never a fault of the mind, ho

but the venerable poet, wishing to send regrets: I met a
fellow once, he says, to the friend in Moose Jaw,
anonymous, practiced polygamy; practice makes perfect,
he claimed

and a peaceable kingdom

but I, naturally enough, was the first man she knew, she
       who loved strawberries next, with cream, then a man
       with a camera for a nose, then adverbs
and loved them faithfully, all or at once or in turn;
       what fit, fit to a т
but now she's in love with butterfly eggs, she sits on
       a clutch of broody eggs
and knits an afghan, asking
but why is the pain so beautiful, the sky so deep, the
       man in the moon

and　I'm hardly the same myself, granted
but　stiff-necked women make me uneasy, I'll admit it
　　　straight out, I'm quiet, I mind my own business
and　the gopher lay down with the hawk, the cabbage plant
　　　with the cutworm
but　then, consider, I'm afflicted with common sense, the
　　　picture of decency, I, hard-working, dedicated,
　　　running over with the milk of whatever, generous
　　　even to a fault, gentle with horses
and　with friends resembling the far end of same
but　fair play, that's my motto; I'm first to put out the
　　　cat, not one to lie down on the job, except of course,
　　　ho; given to elevated thoughts, careful never to
　　　slurp soup, surprised by the stains in my clean
　　　shorts, a drinker who knows his limits, a whist
　　　player of some repute, a lifelong student of
　　　Empedocles, the last of a dying breed, embarrassed
　　　though not exhausted by too frequent masturbation,
　　　a crackerjack at the two-step, unpedantic, slow to
　　　anger, a decorous farter, respectful of my elders,
　　　even when they haven't got all their marbles
　and　a good listener

but   there are limits, you know: down there in upstate New
        York, she with a basket on her bench, she posts a
        sign, garage sale
and all her Saturday, longing: o button of gold, he loves
        me not
but   that's another problem, sleep wears me out these days,
        I wake up tired
and button of bone, of hoof, of horn, please bury the
        dead; he loves me not, he loves me not
but   she's barking up the wrong tree
and button of seed, of shell, o button of linen, button
        of patent leather; he loves my arms in the sun, he
        loves the circle of my hair; o button of bronze, of
        opal, of amber; o button of jade or iron, hoard
        happiness, honor the past, buy government bonds
but   his, the piratical self, is thief
and thieving: o button of braid, of brass, she loves me;
        of quartz, of silver, of pewter or wood; o button or
        hole or hook, she loves me now, she loves me; o button
        of celluloid, she loves me not, of sapphire, she loves
        me, of paper, of paste, she loves me not, of
        mother-of-pearl, she loves me, of tin, of polyester,
        tell us the whole truth
but   hide what must be hidden

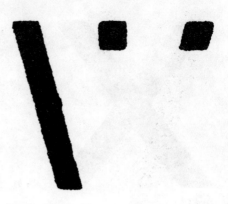

and   if the hook fits the eye, madam, whoop-de-doo; the
        old button-plucker, neither does she, nor, having
        done it, say the word; may her first buttonhole be
        her last, the worm gets hungry too, love
but   I remember the taste of sunset, the cargo all below
        deck, the whiff on the sultry air
and   no feasting allowed: the ox, the crane, c as in fig,
        D for door; hieroglyph to no man, he; the horned
        asp
but   don't be embarrassed, we all wear them; G, in outline,
        the camel's head
and   neck, carry on; hanky-pank, all hail; aye, the law
        had the goods on me from the start; ho, skip it, the
        wine bowl empty, no goading at the harried gate
but   dear Miss Reading saw it, the owl, a rising out
        of Montreal; to wit, the city burning, the city,
        burned in the snowing night
and   here in the west she writes me, please, I carried
        the torch for her, ha, could you send one burrowing
        owl, postpaid, I have found a hole in the mountain;
        no more the arctic dream; the Metro, if you don't
        mind
but   he, a fishy business, that, the hooked eye, snitched
        from the nooky night, running his blastfamous poem
        to halt, who goes there, speak
and   ready to call it quits

but the woman from Nanaimo, she who lives in a submarine,
  now she is all for shipwrecks, she loves each
  sinking, the bodies caressing the sand, with tongue
and foot, the clams carouse: deep now she lurks, down;
  ship boards of fir, she announces, to cradle the
  broken sea; a cedar, O Sad Phoenician, to make thee
  a mast
but keep an ear cocked for sirens, you one-eyed mariner
and the pole star pointing you in, fresh from the coast
  of Ampersand, a cargo to Upsilon bound, the calmest
  cove, the engraving sea, hmmm, yummy, the sacker
  said: two of those, please, the big ones
but wait, don't wrap them, ha

and	yes, there was, somewhere, a tree, he saw, Who?him
but	you're out of it, the lady said, she was very polite,
	she wore a chair on her head, a basket between her
	knees full of salmon; a butterfly almost the shade
	of a Baltimore oriole licked its perfect proboscis
	to her right nipple: she was the guardian of the
	tree, that was clear
and	the tree itself stood in the distance behind her,
	possibly green, possibly not a tree at all, a sail,
	slumped in the windless air, or only a gallows hung
	with sleep
but	why? Who?him, to the palm that either reached or
	resisted
and	she, a tongue like a wick: whoa, there, horse,
	where's the fire
but	he was as ornery as the day: Pythagoras, he said,
	is the name, playing a long shot; he paused
and	was more than a little disappointed; sir, she said,
	I'll take your word
but	I should tell you, twisting a few of the rings on her
	fingers, you've just, in that case, wiseacre, died
and	she meant it

but   Who?him didn't know izzard from A, his donkey from
a hole in the ground, aleph or end, he was all gall,
ho; it's a disguise, he ventured

and   that's when the old gal grinned, where the hell you
been, Phoney; she tapped the butterfly tighter, it
was falling down on the job: I know you're slow

but   what took you, if you'll pardon the expression, so
long

and   one more thing, she continued, an egg in her navel
the size of a fist, about your friend, Pythagoras

but   a salmon leapt out of the basket; she caught it,
quick as a flash

and   a bird lit on her bare left shoulder, a long-legged
squawk, out of nowhere: true, it said, swell, okay,
got you, dead on, man, right, we're doing it now,
hang in

but   the tree was not an inch closer. If it was a tree.
The light was too bright for seeing, green became
blue. Or vice versa.

The Silent
Poet Sequence

The Silent Poet Sees Red

and   green too, on occasion, granted
but   I wouldn't slander a friend for the world, cross
       my heart
and   spit to die
but   he shuts off his inboard motor, he sprawls on the
       deck of his cottage, nursing a beer, he forgets to
       shave for a week
and   he thinks he's a sailor, Earache the Red; it was he
       who discovered dry land
but   sit yourself down, he promises, life is short
and   while you're up, crack us a couple of cold ones,
       poet
but   I hardly have time, he talks too much; he is Professor
       of Nowhere at some place or other; puck, he says,
       waving a stick
and   he skates his way through class, defying entropy,
       slamming the puck under the chairs of his sleeping
       students
but   women are fooled by his library, ha; he's all show;
       may he rupture himself, clipping his toenails
and   while I'm on the subject, his wife has four arms,
       she holds him together, blind as love
but   remember, the pupil is black, we see with darkness
       only
and   I watch for a light in the west, occidents will
       happen, ho
but   sunrise comes at noon to her bed
and   what do we have for lunch, breakfast; Silent Poet,
       she tells me, you are the great keeper, the wellspring
       of was, the guardian of ought
but   that's your loss, not mine
and   soft as blue she whispers a pip into her palm; west
       is a color of the wind

The Silent Poet Moves His Office

but I can't throw this away
and the Maalox, god knows I'll need that; some lead for
     a pencil, ha, well
but the keys; okay, so what if a door does come knocking
and this paper knife, tarnished almost black, Watzernaym
     left it, open the mail, she said, I send you
but she must have forgot
and the English penny that didn't bring luck
but Earache the Red appears in my doorway, gives me the
     willies; ho, he says, caught you
and I'm guilty, I blush; surreptitiously I check my
     fly; saw the boxes out in the hall
but what, he adds, exactly, is the function of objects,
     if you don't mind my asking
and he answers, waving a book, this yours by any chance
but I'm holding a packet of papers, the band breaks,
     the rubber is old
and I pick up a letter, from a patient in the asylum;
     you love me, she says, I can tell by your poems; the
     broken draft of her address, there in the corner; I
     was going to scrawl her a note, a quick apology
     even, maybe send her something
but I open the Maalox
and Earache the Red is shouting, the blur in his hand a
     mousetrap, the blood confused me, in the wire frame,
     the staring eyes; we transfer memory, he
     predicates; more easily put, we chicken
but I take the book, words that I've never seen before,
     underlined by my assertion
and Earache the Red is raving, the object is, he says,
     not to object, get it; he peeks out into the hall;
     he farts

but consider, picking up three sticks of chalk; he
     points; consider this ruler you've carried with
     you, from boyhood on; this embarrassing print of
     a rapids you never hang, this tape you haven't the
     courage to hear; consider, my friend; he points;
     this homemade valentine, this pair of scissors,
     this rock
and I think to myself, I'm sorry, forgive me, I didn't
     mean it
but I go down the hall, my wrists in pain, carrying
     everything

The Silent Poet at Intermission

but who are all these strangers, I ask
and I mean it, heading for the bar
but trust my luck, Earache the Red, a drink in either
     hand, announces, Madame Sosostris has a bad cold this
     evening, we laugh
and I say, that's pharoah enough
but nobody gets it, I buy my own
and Earache, the crowd gathering, art should instruct,
     he tells us, glancing at his reflection
but not by painting the rainbow black, we laugh
and I have a pot myself, Labatt's did that much for me
but she who loves gold loves elsewhere
and follows the path prophesying no end, it's hardly hard
     to guess; uppie uppie, she says in the morning, the
     medium well done
but he hands her a glass, she looks; here's mud in your
     eye
and even The Virgin Queen, she wasn't Shakespeare either
But I did scorn them all, she wrote
and with good cause: a leman is a lemon, ha; well, let the
     heads fall
but music, he says, is the mothering lode; he waves his
     arms; he is composing a series of dichotomies for
     violin
and fiddle, the chiseling clod
but he spills his drink
and I wipe my shoe on my cuff; I hear the weasel that sniffs
     the hen, the blood-loud blood in the gutter, the wise
     man strangling on his own; sorry, mum

but he discovers, just then, the split of mind
and body; putting Descartes before the hearse, we laugh
but just as I raise the dagger the buzzer sounds, I am
      left with the thought in my hand
and he takes her elbow in his palm; the new, he tells us,
      straight to our backs, must learn to be old, to learn
      to be new; we scratch ourselves
but follow, as we lead, to the first usher
and I leave for home, bumping knees with a dozen strangers
but never go

The Silent Poet Finds Out

and they'll get me, I know, dread or alive

but I go out at night, with my shovel, I dig deep holes
in the neighbors' lawns

and Earache the Red, at coffee, for god's sake hit the
sack early, he says, you look like you never sleep

but watch those dirty dreams; he winks

and shakes his spoon in my direction

but I don't let on that I understand

and the mayor is offering a reward, some maniac, he claims,
dug a toilet pit, directly in front of City Hall; the
reward is an insult, I'm worth more

but I look at the posters, I'm tempted, poets are not well
paid, I could use the money

and the grave in the bishop's garden, I don't think that was
mine, I never dig graves

but isn't that the truth, they see what they believe, people,
I go out at night, I dig deep holes

and a friend, late for a meeting, fell headlong into a gap
in the campus green

but didn't smile

and I was alone again in the world

but Earache, there's a new law, he says, you're legally
responsible for all your dreams

and I buy his coffee

but just last night, while he snored in her arms, I pitched
black dirt at his window

and walled him in

but he doesn't let on; he calls for a refill; I'm sweating

and he looks at the morning paper, then looks at me; in
China they've picked up a signal, I wait

but he takes three sugars, I hate that about him; quick
energy, he says; he winks

and I hide my blisters under the table

The Silent Poet Craves Immortality

and even black has its lighter moments, ha

but the doggerel of the sun is such, we stare blankly

and I stop criticizing my friends, I praise their ugly
faces, their staggering poems

but they agree

and then I wonder at my own judgment; I nod; they slap
my back, you've mellowed

but that makes it worse, I watch TV

and memorize the weather, promising, first thing in the
morning, I'll write the last line

but secretly at night I turn signs around, I point
all travelers in the wrong direction; I've so far
derailed three trains; I look at bridges malignantly

and pray with the first two fingers of each hand crossed

but she, in the bathroom, washing between her legs, what
are you doing on your knees

and I leap up

but I think I'm preparing to die, I can smell food inside
a closed fridge, the milk a little sour, the onions
gone soft, as in a wet garden, the hamburger practicing
green

and I bought new dishes yesterday, bright plates, Italian,
flowers on a white background, six Japanese bowls, I
can taste the roses

but cheap, something you could stack in a tomb, send out
on the water

and Jezebel, she sees I'm reading in bed, I study maps,
this is Alberta, I look for rivers that trail off into
dotted lines, this is the Yucatan, this the Siberian
forest; I peruse a linguistic atlas, looking for one word

but she knows I'm watching; she lifts a foot into the
basin, slow as sin

and I put in a bid for a ship, a rust-eaten tanker, nothing
pretentious

but something, nevertheless, that will burn with a flare, ho

and give a signature to the sky

The Silent Poet Eats His Words

but whatever you do, don't

and remember, forget what I said about Watzernaym, miss or
     hit, she didn't love me

but not in the way I wanted not to be loved, I've had enough

and that's only a start, she was an admirer of bricks, she
     liked their fired faces, their false

but predictable ends

and darkness itself she would nothing

but praise, it falls, she said, not like you, feigning a
     light

and I learned to hate from her loving, her ink pot, calling
     the letter back; I teased her awake

but touch your typewriter, poet, she whispered, then I can
     sleep in the morning

and that was a hard one to swallow, ho; I tried for an hour

but life is a series, I explained, I drew diagrams on the
     frosted window, I brushed the wrinkles from the sheet
     where I wanted her to lie

and after another failure I stood, delicately, on my own
     head, defying her to tell up from down; love, I said,
     I'm inclined to agree

but the penny saved is, generally, lost; a stitch in time
     seams nothing, ha

and I argued, at length, for the inevitable rise of the
     real, into Idea; this time it's forever, I added

but all my blood sank to my brain, I was left hanging, my
     neck hurt; I was trying to amuse

and Ahab, I said, was a fool to marry you, Jezebel

but don't feel bad, I'm depressed myself, there's a flock
      of two thousand birds that shits on my car, they sit
      in this saskatoon bush, see, waiting
and when I drive up the leader says, shit
but sometimes I fool them; I hesitate; just as I open the
      door
and after they've all obeyed the command, like the stooges
      they are, I step out, regally, majestically, I step from
      the car, I bow, just slightly; Francis, I say, is the
      name; skip the saint business
but she was sound asleep, except for a rhythmic snoring,
      suggesting she might be awake; please, she said, jerking
      the covers from the place where I might have been, read
      the review of your book again, make some coffee, scrub
      that goddamn kitchen floor, vacuum, take your pulse,
      fix the toaster, go put on your snow tires, asshole,
      it's January

The
Winnipeg
Zoo

The Winnipeg Zoo

yes, I am here, exhausted, a wreck, unable
to imagine the act of writing, unable to imagine

I am here, it is quiet, I am exhausted from
moving, we must take care of our stories

the moving is a story, we must take care, I am
here, I shall arrive, I am arriving, I too

have waited, the way in is merely the way,
she takes her lovers, reader, listen, be careful

she takes her lovers one by one to the Winnipeg
zoo, she winds her hair on her fingers, the hook

in the ceiling holds the plant, the ivy climbs
to the floor, must is the end

of winter, the ride to the zoo, the sun on the
man at the gate, the hair wound on her fingers

she takes her lovers, first, the startled boy
stares at the pink flamingos, they rest, folding

one leg at a time, the standing boy, she returns
alone from the Winnipeg zoo, her brown eyes

misting into calm, the hook in the ceiling
holds the plant, what matters is all that matters

the man at the gate says nothing, the kiss of
the Canada lynx, the lightning touch of the snake

is hot, love is round, thumbs are still fingers,
we must take care of our stories, the reptiles

waiting, do not move, flamingos have no names,
the boy, the tall young man, reaching to find her

hand, the polar bear dives deep, into the coiling
water, Audubon raises his gun, the artist

the owl is master of sleep, don't follow,
she takes her lovers past the pond

the farmer from Delacroix, the one who grows
asparagus spears, the one who feeds gourmands

is watching the reptiles, he does not move,
we must take care of our stories, or what it is

is only this, thumbs are still fingers, always,
after an early lunch, the zoological garden

the secret is in the ketchup bottle, the farmer
has short toes, red hair, he wears blue shoes

the man at the gate is not counting, a trickle of
gold at her neck, no wind, her scattered love

is round, Audubon raises his gun, the cranes
reply to the wild turkeys, always, after

an early lunch, the farmer, his hands to the glass,
it is quiet, reader, listen, she comes back alone

flamingoes have no names, monkeys learn by hanging,
the lawyer, cracking sunflower seeds, spits

at the watching tiger, he reaches to take
her hand, the popcorn vender winks

at a scalding baby, somewhere, rococo,
a killdeer furrows the air, the lawyer

cracking sunflower seeds, spits at the tiger's
yellow eyes, but cannot quite imagine

the artist, Audubon, dipping the beaded sight
into the flattened V on the gun's barrel, we must

take care, the sun is a fish,
monkeys learn by hanging, the lizard is only

half asleep, write on the post card, quickly,
I am here, yes, I want to go home, the man

at the gate is not counting, Audubon dips the
beaded sight into the flattened V on the gun's

barrel, the lawyer, cracking sunflower seeds,
the tiger blinks, politely, I am here

exhausted, she is with me, the artist,
Audubon, tightens his index finger

her eyes mist into a calm, the elk
in the distant pasture raises his rack

then it is done, the ducks in the duck pond
cannot fly, the sun sticks out its shadow

we must take care of our stories, I am ex-
hausted from moving, it is quiet, I am here

Sketches

Of A

Lemon

Sketches of a Lemon

1.

A lemon is almost round.
Some lemons are almost round.
A lemon is not round.

So much for that.

How can one argue that a lemon
is truly a lemon,
if the question can be argued?

So much for that.

I said, to Smaro
(I was working on this poem),
Smaro, I called, is there
(she was in the kitchen)
a lemon in the fridge?
No, she said.

So much for that.

2.

As my father used to say,
well I'll be cow-kicked
by a mule.

He was especially fond of
lemon meringue pie.

3.

I went and looked at Francis Ponge's poem
on blackberries. If blackberries can be
blackberries, I reasoned, by a kind of analogy,
lemons can, I would suppose, be lemons.

Such was not the case.

4.

Sketches, I reminded myself,
not of a pear,
nor of an apple,
nor of a peach,
nor of a banana
(though the colour
raises questions),
nor of a nectarine,
nor, for that matter,
of a pomegranate,
nor of three cherries,
their stems joined,
nor of a plum,
nor of an apricot,
nor of the usual
bunch of grapes,
fresh from the vine,
just harvested,
glistening with dew —

Smaro, I called,
I'm hungry.

5.

What about oranges?
At least an orange
looks like an orange.
In fact, most oranges
bear a remarkable resemblance
to oranges.

6.

Smaro is rolling a lemon on the breadboard.
The breadboard, flat, horizontal, is motionless.
The lemon rolls back and forth on the motionless surface.
Smaro's hand moves horizontally, back and forth,
over the rolling lemon.

One could draw a diagram of the three related objects,
deduce therefrom a number of mechanical principles.

7.

I had a very strong desire
to kiss a lemon.
No one was watching.
I kissed a lemon.

So much for that.

8.

I bought a second-hand car —
Okay, okay.

9.

If someone asked me,
how is a lemon shaped?

       (the salmon
       (the oven
       (the lemon

I'd say, a lemon is shaped
exactly like an hour.

(Now we're getting somewhere.)

10.

The lemon cure.
In each glass
mix: 1 stick cinnamon
       1 teaspoon honey
       2 cloves
       2 jiggers rum
       ½ slice lemon
       hot water to taste

Repeat as necessary.

11.

poem for a child who has just bit into
a halved lemon that has just been squeezed:

    see, what did I tell you, see,
    what did I tell you, see, what
    did I tell you, see, what did
    I tell you, see, what did I
    tell you, see, what did I tell
    you, see, what did I tell you,
    see, what did I tell you, see,
    what did I tell you, see, what
    did I tell you, see, what did
    I tell you, see, what did I
    tell you, see, what did I tell
    you, see, what did I tell you

One could, of course, go on.

12.

This hour is shaped like
a lemon.   We taste its light

on the baked salmon.
The tree itself is elsewhere.

We make faces, liking the
sour surprise. Our teeth melt.

The Criminal
Intensities
Of Love
As
Paradise

'Morning, Jasper Park'

etymologies
of sun or
stone of ear
and listening

the bent of
birth on edge
the chrysalis
and parting bone

old as old as
time as time   *hearing*
holding   *footfalls*
hand of hand   *that must*
                      be those
& ripe as rite   .   *of a bear*
the dreamers
dreaming
feet or foot

of lodgepole &
a bear below   *the lovers*
bellow   *awake*
a nose   *in their*
                      tent
jay song   *in the*
and scolding   *forest*
timpani to
skald of scene

the once upon
the figurine
of eye
insinuating

the is of light
is all or all
the ending of
the lip on lip

'Fire & Pan'

similitude
of fire waits
as always as
a waltz

this stopping of
must now go on
an axe to axiom
or folded arm

cripes a killed   *the lovers*
god or still
the scanning ear
astray or astral

or nickelodeon
of beast & bird   *debating*
a thrust of thumb   *who shall*
cretaceous   *remain in the*
                                   sleeping bag
in eiderdown the   *who*
labyrinth of belly   *crawl out*
beg or theseus   *to kindle*
& bully too   *a fire*

the luting pan
unscramble skull
or chipmunk
wittgenstein

as wind is
metaphysical   *quarrel*
a tree so slowly
lays its eggs

lovers have hold
of hold and
turn and turn
the flapjack mind

'Breakfast, After, & Looking'

      in which
      the lovers

      leaving their
      breakfast dishes
      to soak in a
or even elk   *yellow plastic*
in elk meadow *pail*
or forest
allowing tree   *walk towards*
      the distant
hello & hollow *falls*
how
the knocking knuckle
knocks

perfect as
spoon or pillow
was or would or
willow bunch

the bell
ringing the bell
the cryptic message
in the scar

profanely lucid
fall or hail
the mountain
all alone alone

ride or riddance
to the last field
radiance of
washed rock

risking the
loud fever
roses and red
& violets

to make a song
to make a song
the folding water
feed the eye

'Standing Near a Waterfall'

the torque of
absolute desire
river & the wind
arouse

as rounded as
a hat the head
so quickly now
and O so clean

or wind or wind
of memorizing
dark the drop
of spanking stone

bent & the break
and then comes
after after
the reaching sea

the lunar patterns
of the mind
and horse beware
the horse

there being
a ledge handy
the lovers
standing

as fetal as
precambrian
or harlequin to
stopped throat

upon it
consider
the usual
lovers' leap

or yet the hand
unarmed unharmed
return
& cinquefoil bloom

or fountain wild
of jack & jill
the maelstrom of
and columbine

O this is where
the raven fell
& this is where
the raven fell

'Salt, of Ocean Sea, of Tears'

the forfeiture
of ending
to begin begin
& arch & heel

the tent's hot
light
or flagging or
the caved eye   *having*
                                     narrowly
the finding hand   *avoided*
or mouthing &   *death*
the salted sea
open and trade   *the lovers*
                                     return to
a new america   *their tent*
pepper & tears   *intending*
or heraclitus if   *to have*
skulduggery
                                     a quickie
the darting of
& tongue & tongue
sheet or heat of
lightning

cry out & cry
white
as alabaster is
or dipping gull

to god or after
and a portraiture
of merely is
or queen of spain

'Awoken and, Again, Hungry, Again'

& death as proud
as death
or harping amphion
arouse a wall

the lovers
while eating
a bologna sandwich
and drinking
the first beer
of the day
hold discourse
as to which

ankle or calf
annihilate
the back of knee
recite racine

of all their
zones
is most
erogenous

or moose rutting
or mossy ear
the atavistic
buttock bare

becoming of
of teeth
to peeled root
or onion even

but belly
button best
lending
& all directions

'Into Town'

whole wheat or
rye or 2 %
or skim
riddle the take

or taco stand
arise arise
& soft ice cream
& zero meet

or zeno
one white lie
tucking to heart
the arrow's nib

the bandit tree
or ashtray sign
decorum and its
data cross

on floor on
floor or mall
or siwash
melt the feet

far & the rattle
meet the bear &
norse nor apple
plastic head

and then
the lovers
decide that
instead of
driving up to
the columbia
icefields to
spend the day
taking pictures
or maybe hiking
they'll zip
into town
for a loaf
of bread and
some milk
and maybe
even a
jug of
donini

'Post Card to a Hillside'

sunwapta &
or athabasca
or the sliding
in interior

a post card to
the raven's beak
and lovers' eyes
are taller now

the lovers
stop
to look
at the

antipodes of
everywhere
explode the
book of hours

totem pole
by the
CN tracks

& post card to
a poet's name
unhook to learn
the rainbow fish

or post card then
to dead
vivaldi
play O play O play

& of & to mt robson
PS hi
where rivers braid
the gelded sand

'Nude Swimmers in Late Afternoon'

& alpha &
a road allowance
& red squirrel
paying crow

guide & end
to nowhere   *mosquitoes*
lost pool &   *be damned*
jaybird white

                       the lovers
waiting & fare   *pull off the*
warning or way   *road and*
blue water &   *likewise*
a wry step   *pull off their*
                       clothes and
& scree & cliff   *go for a*
montane   *swim*
pubic as   *in the buff*
periphery & ah

the ha the hoo
mounting and
dip and deep
hullabalooing

                       shivering

huh & the hee
hieratic
& holy old
& jumping

the plash
and kiss and
wrought hands
roughing

and fescue
grass &
offering
& myriad tongue

'Campsite, Home, Away From'

or tree as roof
and origin
and savaging
the height of hill

& the lost & the
late home always
found
in the small flame

lovers are only
this and more
a cracking stick
a mortal sun

or fish or bird
or beast
and a black pot   *smoke rising*
and fire fending   *from numerous*
                         fires

the ikon element
the scalp
reminding   *children*
cheese & wine   *at play*

and barking at
a dog a dog   *the camp*
or venus maybe   *busy*
or baked beans

                         and campers
                         asking
                         each other
                         where
                         they are
                         from

'Bear Story with or without Bear'

& the knicknack
day done &   *the lovers*
night & night   *turn off*
or a pocket moon   *the coleman*
                         lantern
& after the least   *and then*
page or last   *quickly*
coals fanned   *crawl into*
passage & end   *the sack*

or tent flap &
the forecast low
forest & fain
& would lie down

and lie awake

listening

rank as the rank
scenting of bear
bear baiting
breath

catching & bruit
enactment
far or fury
wizarding fear

and in the arms
and arms of and
a creature or
O creaking wind

both & both &
drifting to
or holding
lapidary dark

wisp of the
toldtale
midnight
teller & arrive

'And Dreamers, Even Then, if Dreaming'

over the chained
mountain
the ridebound eagle
risk & tame

& hover the long
wings waived
& wide as wide
as sleep

eerie & enter
if
& the pale garden
chill as white

and now
the lovers
find
the perfect
glacier
of all

or stalled in
draglong and
the pitchfall
slide

their
once
ambitions

the storm
commencing seed
the spider
reach

albino night
to extricate
the called
grammarian

the closed eye
listen &
O nesting tongue
hatch the world